W9-COY-752

I Belong to the Christian Faith

Katie Dicker and Sam Dilkes

PowerKiDS
press.

New York

Published in 2010 by The Rosen Publishing Group Inc.
29 East 21st Street, New York, NY 10010

First Edition

Library of Congress Cataloging-in-Publication Data

Dicker, Katie.
  I belong to the Christian faith / Katie Dicker and Sam Dilkes.
     p. cm. -- (I belong)
  Includes index.
  ISBN 978-1-4358-3032-5 (library binding)
  ISBN 978-1-4358-8618-6 (paperback)
  ISBN 978-1-4358-8619-3 (6-pack)
  1. Christian life--Juvenile literature. I. Dilkes, Sam II. Title.
  BV4501.3.D54 2010
  230--dc22
                              2008051874

Manufactured in China

Disclaimer
The text in this book is based on the experience of one family. Although every effort
has been made to offer accurate and clearly expressed information, the author and
publisher acknowledge that some explanations may not be relevant to those who
practice their faith in a different way.

Acknowledgements
The author and publisher would like to thank the following people for their help and
participation in this book:
The Dilkes family and Rev. Danny Wignall.

Photography by Chris Fairclough.

In memory of Jill Dilkes
A loving mother to Hannah, Molly, and Sam.

Contents

My family

Hi, I'm Sam, and this is my family—my mom and dad and my sisters, Hannah and Molly. We're Christians. Today it's Sunday and we're going to **church** in town.

Mom and Dad don't work on Sundays, so we can all spend the day together.

We go to church to **worship** God, who created the world. God lives in **heaven**, but he lives inside me, too, because God is everywhere.

Our church is nearby, so we can walk there. The church has a big **steeple**, which points to heaven.

Going to church

At church, we sit down and listen to a **sermon** by the **vicar**. He tells us about God and about a man called Jesus. I like the vicar. He knows a lot of things and he makes us laugh.

The vicar wears a white collar. We call it a dog collar. It goes around his neck, but it doesn't have a leash!

We also sing **hymns** and songs to show how much we love God. We sing about all the things in the world God has given us, and we thank God for looking after us.

Sometimes, I go up to the front of the church with my friends to sing songs we have learned.

Who is Jesus?

God sent Jesus to live on earth about 2,000 years ago. Jesus taught people about God and how to live a good life. But some people did not like Jesus. They nailed him on a cross to die.

This statue shows Jesus on the cross. It must have been an awful way to die.

TO THOSE OF THIS
IN THE WARS
THEIR NAME LIVETH

PARISH WHO FELL
OF 1914-18 · 1939-45
FOR EVERMORE

1945
SLEY
RKE
DER
LL
ES
F
BRIDGE
RTH

C. BARKVILL
H. BARKVILL
C. BRIMLEY
J. CLAPSHAW
W. CRESSWELL
H. CRESSWELL
C. CROWTHER
F. EDGELER
A. ELLIOT
F. MADGWICK

C. FROGLEY
J. HARDING
F. V. HARDING
G. A. HERVEY
W. HOOPER
H. HOY
C. JUDGE
W. LEMON
V. LUFF

W. MOORE
M. NEWMAN
C. NIGHTINGALE
P. RAPSON
W. ROBINSON
C. SELWYN
A. P. SELWYN
G. V. C. SELWYN
W. SHORT

W. SNELLING
J. SNELLING
A. STEER
H. TOWELL
B. WHITE
W. WOOD
B. WOOD
C. WOOD
J. VOLLER

1939
E.A.
B
V
P
G RE
S.F
J.R.B. SI
J.H.W

Although Jesus died, God brought him back to life again after three days. It was a **miracle**! Jesus taught us that if we believe in God, we will also be given new life and will be with him when we die.

I wear this cross to show that I am a Christian. I have a few cross necklaces, but this is my favorite— I like the color.

Communion

Before Jesus died, he had supper with the **disciples**. Jesus told his friends he would always be with them. There is a big table at the front of the church called the altar. It reminds us of this meal.

The vicar stands behind the altar and holds up some bread and wine.

At church, we go up to the altar to share the bread and wine. We call it **communion**. We eat and drink to remember that although Jesus died, he will always be with us.

The vicar gives me bread and wine. I feel sad when I think that Jesus died for us.

Sunday school

I go to Sunday school with my friends. We do drama and read **Bible** stories. Sometimes, we do craft activities. It's a lot of fun—we learn about God and about Jesus, but we have time to play, too.

Today, we're listening to a story about life in heaven. We're talking about what it means to us.

We learn about the way Jesus was patient and kind to other people. If we follow what Jesus says, we can talk to him like a friend and do the things he did to make other people's lives better.

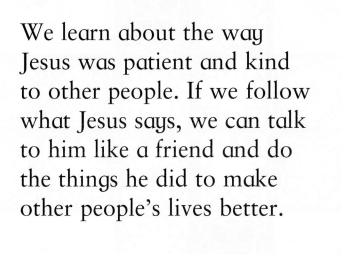

These words describe how we can be more like Jesus. We are putting the words on a "tree of life," so everyone else can see them.

Getting to know God

We pray to thank God for all the good things in our life. At the end of a **prayer**, we say "Amen." This means "I agree" and tells God we really mean what we have said.

Every night, Mom **blesses** me and we say a prayer together. We also ask God to help if we are worried about something.

The Bible is a book full of stories about God and about Jesus. My favorite stories tell us how God made the world, and how Jesus was born in a stable.

I try to read some of the Bible every night, to learn about God and the best way to live.

Praying

Last year, Mom wasn't very well. Lots of people at church prayed for her. Mom is a lot better now. We think that God heard everyone praying and helped to make her well again.

These are some of our friends at church. When Mom was sick, everyone was thinking about her.

We say prayers for someone we know who is unwell, or for people in the world who are hungry or poor. We pray that their lives will get better and that they will get to know Jesus as a friend, too.

We light candles at church. We do this to pray for other people and to remind us that God is always near.

Living a good life

Jesus taught us to try to be good people. I try to share things with my sisters and to be kind to them. Sometimes it's hard, but I do my best.

My room can get a bit messy. I straighten and vacuum so that Mom doesn't have to.

If we believe in Jesus and behave like him, God will look after us when we die. It's hard to be good all the time, but God gives us a second chance if we say sorry for something we have done wrong.

Dad was angry when I broke this ornament, but because he loves me, he forgave me when I said sorry.

Christian festivals

In December, we celebrate **Christmas**. This is when Jesus was born. We have a big family meal at home and we give each other presents. God gave Jesus as a gift to the world, so we like to give presents, too.

On Christmas, we put this nativity scene out at home. It reminds us of all the people who came to see the baby Jesus.

Easter is a very special celebration in the springtime. We remember the time that Jesus came back to life again. We go to church to celebrate and we eat chocolate and candy Easter eggs when we come home!

I help Mom make an Easter garden every year. It's really pretty. We add stones to show where Jesus was buried.

Glossary, further information, and Web Sites

Bible a special book full of stories about God and Jesus.

bless to ask God to look after something or someone.

church a building where Christians go to worship God.

communion the sharing of bread and wine during a Christian service.

disciples the friends of Jesus who followed his teaching.

heaven the place where God lives.

hymns songs that worship God.

miracle an amazing event.

prayer a way of talking to God.

sermon a religious talk.

steeple a pointed roof.

vicar a person who leads Anglican worship.

worship to show love and respect to God.

Did you know?

- There are over two billion Christians around the world.
- The word *Christianity* comes from "Christ," which means "someone God has chosen."
- There are different types of Christians, such as Anglicans, Roman Catholics, Baptists, Methodists, and Lutherans.
- Sunday is a special day of prayer for Christians, because Jesus came back to life on a Sunday.

Activities

1. Plan to visit a local church. How many symbols of the cross can you find at the church?
2. Do you know any hymns? Try to find the words to a famous hymn. What is it about?
3. Read a story from the Bible and draw a picture to show part of this story.

Books to read

- *Rookie Read-About Holidays: Easter* by David F. Marx (Children's Press, 2001)

- *This is my Faith: Christianity* by Anita Ganeri (Barron's Educational, 2006)

- *What You Will See Inside A Catholic Church* by Michael Keane (Skylight Paths Publishing, 2002)

Web Sites

Due to the changing nature of Internet links, PowerKids Press has developed an online list of Web sites related to the subject of this book. This site is updated regularly. Please use this link to access this list: www.powerkidslinks.com/blong/christ

Christian festivals

Advent (December)
A time before Christmas when Christians look forward to the birth of Jesus.

Christmas (December 25)
A festival celebrating the birth of Jesus.

Easter (March/April)
A festival to celebrate the fact that when Jesus died, he came back to life again.

Pentecost (May/June)
A celebration of the day that God sent his holy spirit to the disciples, to help them to teach other people about God.

Harvest home (September/October)
A festival to thank God for providing the food that people need to live.

Christian symbols

Cross a symbol to show the way that Jesus died.

Egg a symbol of new life.

Fish many of Jesus' disciples were fishermen, and a fish was used as a secret symbol of the church long ago.

Index

A
altar 10, 11

B
Bible 12, 15, 22
blessing 14, 22

C
candle 17
Christmas 20, 23
church 4, 5, 6, 10, 11, 16,
  17, 21, 22
communion 10, 11, 22
cross 8, 9, 23

D
death 8, 9, 11, 19
disciples 10, 22

E
Easter 21, 23

F
family 4, 5, 18, 19, 20
festivals 20, 21, 23
forgiveness 19
friends 7, 12, 13, 16, 17

G
God 5, 6, 7, 8, 9, 12, 14, 15,
  16, 17, 19

H
heaven 5, 12, 22
hymns 7, 22

J
Jesus 6, 8, 9, 10, 11, 12, 13,
  15, 17, 18, 19, 20, 21

K
kindness 13, 18

M
miracle 9, 22

P
prayer 14, 16, 17, 22
presents 20

S
sermon 6, 22
steeple 5, 22
Sunday 4
Sunday school 12
symbols 23

V
vicar 6, 10, 11, 22

W
world 5, 7, 15, 17
worship 5, 22